Water Rolls, Water Rises
El agua rueda, el agua sube

Pat Mora

illustrations / *ilustraciones* Meilo So

translation / traducción Adriana Domínguez & Pat Mora

Children's Book Press, *an imprint of* Lee & Low Books Inc.
New York

Water rolls
onto the shore
under the sun, under the moon.

El agua rueda
hacia la orilla
bajo el sol, bajo la luna.

Water rises
into soft fog,
weaves down the street, strokes an old cat.

El agua sube
formando suave neblina
que ondula por la calle, acaricia a un gato viejo.

Blown by the wind,
water sails high.
Tumbling cloud plumes curl through the air.

Soplada por el viento,
el agua se remonta.
Volutas nebulosas ruedan por el aire.

*S*low into rivers,
water slithers and snakes
through silent canyons at twilight and dawn.

Lenta, el agua
se desliza y serpentea hacia los ríos
por cañones silenciosos al anochecer y al amanecer.

Down smooth canals,
water streams, water slides,
gliding up roots of tulips and corn.

Por canales lisos,
el agua fluye y resbala,
subiendo por las raíces de los tulipanes y el maíz.

Filling deep wells,
water hums in the dark,
sloshes in buckets, quenches our thirst.

Llenando hondos pozos,
el agua susurra en la oscuridad,
salpica en baldes, nos apaga la sed.

*S*wirling in wisps,
water twists then it twirls,
frosts scattered dry leaves, rubs lonely, bare trees.

*G*irando en espirales,
el agua se enrosca y se retuerce,
escarcha las hojas caídas, frota los árboles desnudos y solitarios.

In storms, water plunges
in thunder's brash roar,
races through branches from lightning's white flash.

En las tormentas, el agua se sumerge
en el intrépido rugido del trueno,
de rama en rama huye del blanco destello del relámpago.

Then water rests,
drowsy in reservoirs,
its glistening silence shimmers like stars.

Luego el agua descansa,
soñolienta en las represas,
su reluciente silencio resplandece como estrellas.

*I*n the murmur of marsh wind,
water slumbers on moss,
whispers soft songs far under frog feet.

*E*n el viento susurrante de los pantanos,
el agua duerme sobre el musgo,
murmura suaves canciones bajo patitas de ranas.

Water burbles in springs,
gurgles and turns
down streams and rivers seeking the sea.

El agua burbujea en los manantiales,
borbotea y desciende
por los arroyos y ríos buscando el mar.

*S*kidding and slipping,
swooping round bends,
spinning on tree roots, careening down cliffs.

*P*atinando y resbalando,
corriendo por las curvas,
rotando por raíces, cayendo de barrancos.

Looping and leaping,
rushing to dive
into glimmering sea waves, spangle and splash.

Circulando y brincando,
hasta zambullirse
en centelleantes olas, reluce y ¡paf!, estalla.

*A*round our round world,
water rolls, water rises
under gold sun, under white moon.

*R*odeando nuestro redondo mundo,
el agua rueda, el agua sube
bajo el dorado sol, bajo la blanca luna.

Author's Note

Water fascinates me, perhaps because I've spent most of my life in the Southwest desert region of the United States. The sound of rain is welcome music on a dry and thirsty landscape. Creeks and rivers refresh desert dwellers, and lakes—so much water—seem a surprise. Lightning and downpours startle. Snow softens mountains, hills, cactuses, rocks.

I've also had the good fortune to travel to and savor varied landscapes, cultures, and water features in the United States, and in India, China, Holland, Peru, Finland, Canada, Greece, and Mexico. Oceans always astound me. I've marveled at grand waterways and at children splashing in pools and brooks.

Water—essential, cleansing, dramatic, soothing—is a research interest of my husband, Vern Scarborough, a professor of archaeology. I have benefited from his knowledge, and also from his enthusiasm about the wonder of water and the importance of valuing this glorious natural resource.

Nota de la autora

El agua me fascina, quizás porque he pasado la mayor parte de mi vida en el desierto del suroeste de los Estados Unidos. El sonido de la lluvia parece una agradable melodía cuando cae sobre un paisaje tan árido y sediento. Los arroyos y ríos refrescan a los habitantes del desierto, y los lagos —tanta agua— son una sorpresa. Los relámpagos y aguaceros asustan. La nieve suaviza montañas, cerros, cactos, rocas.

He tenido la buena fortuna de viajar y disfrutar de una variedad de paisajes, culturas y cuerpos de agua en los Estados Unidos y en India, China, Holanda, Perú, Finlandia, Canadá, Grecia y México. Los océanos siempre me asombran. Me he maravillado ante imponentes canales, y ante niños chapoteando en charcas y arroyos.

El agua —esa sustancia esencial, purificadora, dramática, relajante— es tema de estudio de mi esposo, Vern Scarborough, quien es profesor de arqueología. Me ha beneficiado su conocimiento y también su entusiasmo sobre la maravilla que es el agua y sobre la importancia de valorar este magnífico recurso natural.

About the Images in the Book / Sobre las imágenes en el libro

Inspired by Victoria Falls, on the border of Zambia and Zimbabwe

Inspirada por las cataratas Victoria, en la frontera entre Zambia y Zimbabue

Inspired by Strokkur, a geyser in Iceland

Inspirada por Strokkur, un géiser que se encuentra en Islandia

Inspired by the coast of northern California, USA

Inspirada por la costa del norte de California, EE.UU.

Inspired by the Grand Canal, Venice, Italy

Inspirada por el Gran Canal, Venecia, Italia

Inspired by fishing boats off the coast of Goa, India

Inspirada por barcos de pesca en la costa de Goa, India

Inspired by Qutang Gorge of the Yangtze River, China

Inspirada por la garganta Qutang del río Yangtsé, China

Inspired by the canals of Holland, the Netherlands

Inspirada por los canales holandeses, Países Bajos

Inspired by rural villages in Kenya

Inspirada por las aldeas rurales de Kenia

Inspired by Urho Kekkonen National Park, Lapland, Finland

Inspirada por el Parque Nacional Urho Kekkonen, Laponia, Finlandia

Inspired by Torres del Paine National Park, Patagonia, Chile

Inspirada por el Parque Nacional Torres del Paine, Patagonia, Chile

Inspired by an oasis in the Sahara, Morocco

Inspirada por un oasis en el Sahara, Marruecos

Inspired by the wild rice harvest in northern Minnesota, USA

Inspirada por la cosecha del arroz silvestre en el norte de Minnesota, EE.UU.

Inspired by a village in Peloponnese, Greece

Inspirada por un pueblo en el Peloponeso, Grecia

Inspired by Grand Canyon National Park, Arizona, USA

Inspirada por el Parque Nacional Gran Cañón, Arizona, EE.UU.

Inspired by the coast of Cabo San Lucas, Baja California, Mexico

Inspirada por la costa de Cabo San Lucas, Baja California, México

Inspired by our blue planet, Earth

Inspirada por nuestro planeta azul, la Tierra

For my husband, Vern Scarborough, a water scholar —P.M.
Para mi esposo, Vern Scarborough, un investigador del agua —P.M.

For Phil Kennerley —M.S.
Para Phil Kennerley —M.S.

Text copyright © 2014 by Pat Mora
Illustrations copyright © 2014 by Meilo So
Spanish translation copyright © 2014 by Lee & Low Books Inc.
All rights reserved. No part of this book may be reproduced, transmitted, or stored
in an information retrieval system in any form or by any means, electronic, mechanical,
photocopying, recording, or otherwise, without written permission from the publisher.
Children's Book Press, an imprint of LEE & LOW BOOKS INC.,
95 Madison Avenue, New York, NY 10016, leeandlow.com
Spanish translation by Adriana Domínguez and Pat Mora
Book design by Christy Hale
Book production by The Kids at Our House
The text is set in Weiss Medium
The illustrations are rendered in mixed media
Manufactured in China by Jade Productions, July 2014
10   9   8   7   6   5   4   3   2   1
First Edition

Library of Congress Cataloging-in-Publication Data
Mora, Pat, author, translator.
Water rolls, water rises / Pat Mora ; illustrations, Meilo So ;
translation, Adriana Domínguez & Pat Mora = El agua rueda, el agua sube / Pat Mora ;
ilustraciones, Meilo So ; traducción, Adriana Domínguez & Pat Mora. — First edition.
pages cm
Summary: "A series of verses, in English and Spanish, about the movement and moods of water
around the world and the ways in which water affects a variety of landscapes and cultures.
Includes Author's Note"— Provided by publisher.
ISBN 978-0-89239-325-1 (hardcover : alk. paper)
[1. Water—Fiction. 2. Spanish language materials—Bilingual.] I. So, Meilo, illustrator.
II. Domínguez, Adriana, translator. III. Title. IV. Title: El agua rueda, el agua sube.
PZ73.M6393 2014
[E]—dc23   2014003435